THE GREAT OUTDOORS

BOWHUNTING

Revised and Updated

by Aileen Weintraub

Consultant:
Marilyn Bentz
Executive Director
National Bowhunter Education Foundation
Fort Smith, Arkansas

Edge Books are published by Capstone Press,
151 Good Counsel Drive, P.O. Box 669, Mankato, Minnesota 56002.
www.capstonepress.com

Printed in the United States of America

Library of Congress Cataloging-in-Publication Data
Weintraub, Aileen, 1973–
Bowhunting / By Aileen Weintraub.—Rev. and updated.
p. cm.—(Edge Books. The great outdoors)
Rev. ed. of: Bow hunting, 2004.
Includes bibliographical references and index.
ISBN-13: 978-1-4296-0814-5 (hardcover)
ISBN-10: 1-4296-0814-5 (hardcover)
1. Bowhunting—Juvenile literature. I. Weintraub, Aileen, 1973– Bow hunting.
II. Title. III. Title: Bow hunting. IV. Series.
SK36.W45 2008
799.2'15—dc22 2007011172

Summary: Discusses the history, needed equipment, and techniques of hunting with a bow and arrow, as well as related safety and conservation issues.

Editorial Credits
James Anderson, editor; Jo Miller, photo researcher; Tom Adamson, revised edition editor; Thomas Emery, revised edition designer; Kyle Grenz, revised edition production designer

Photo Credits
Bruce Coleman Inc./Larry R. Ditto, 5
Capstone Press/Karon Dubke, cover; Gary Sundermeyer, 13, 14, 17, 18, 25, 26, 29, 37,
Corbis/D. Robert & Lorri Franz, 42; Geoffrey Clements, 7; Lowell Georgia, 31; Royalty-Free, 40
Corel, 21, 43, 44, 45
EyeWire Images, 34
Leonard Rue Enterprises, 11, 33
North American Whitetail/Ron Sinfelt, 8
Wade Nolan, AWP, Inc., 23

Capstone Press thanks Tiffani Atherton for her help with the cover image.

1 2 3 4 5 6 12 11 10 09 08 07

TABLE OF CONTENTS

Features

Essential content terms are highlighted and are defined at the bottom of the page where they first appear.

Chapter 1

BOWHUNTING

Learn about the history of bowhunting, early bows, and archery.

People have hunted for food since prehistoric times. Hunting has also been a way of getting fur and leather for clothing. Today, most people don't have to hunt to survive. But hunting is still a popular challenge for those who enjoy the outdoors.

Bowhunting dates back thousands of years. Ancient Egyptians were among the earliest known people to use a bow and arrow to hunt for food.

Later in history, using a bow became a sport. The sport is called archery. In China, people took part in archery games. Archery contests were also popular in England.

Archery continued to be a popular sport in England for many years. It was mainly a sport for wealthy people. Bowhunting became known as the "sport of kings."

archery—the sport of shooting at targets using a bow and arrow

Bowhunters enjoy the challenge of hunting with a bow and arrow.

American Indian Bowhunters

Some American Indian groups hunted with bows and arrows. American Indians had traditional ways of making bows and arrows. Some used the Osage orange tree to make their bows. This tree has thick, strong limbs. The limbs bend easily without breaking. The hickory tree was used for making arrows. Some arrows were also made from bison, deer, and other animal bones.

Some American Indians used tendons from deer or other large animals as string for their bows. Indians cut the tendons into short strands. They tied the strands together to fit the bow.

Bowhunting in the United States

Saxton Pope and Arthur Young are often called the fathers of modern bowhunting. In the early 1900s, they met an American Indian named Ishi. He taught them how to bowhunt.

Aldo Leopold was another early U.S. bowhunter. Leopold helped to create a hunting season for hunters who use a bow

Some American Indians used bows and arrows to hunt bison.

and arrows. This season was separate from rifle hunting season. All states now have bowhunting seasons.

Today, about 3 million people hunt with bows and arrows. Some of these hunters feel closer to nature because they are hunting the way early people did. Bowhunters believe that hunting with a bow and arrows is a challenging sport that takes patience.

Mike Beatty of Ohio poses with his record buck.

On November 8, 2000, Mike Beatty waited quietly 18 feet (5.5 meters) off the ground in a hunting stand. Since he started deer hunting at age 12, Beatty never thought of setting world records. He just always had loved the challenge of hunting wild game.

But that afternoon, he saw the outline of a massive buck. Its enormous antlers curved every which way. When the buck was about 12 yards (11 meters) away, Beatty had a clear shot. He aimed his compound bow and shot the deer in the neck.

The injured deer ran into the brush. Beatty tracked the deer until it was too dark to see.

The next morning, Beatty and his 10-year-old son, Andrew, were back at the hunting spot by dawn. About 30 yards (27 meters) from where Beatty stopped tracking the animal lay the dead buck. Beatty was honored when the 39-point buck was named the world record non-typical white-tailed deer.

EDGE FACT

A non-typical white-tailed deer has unusual antlers. They point in every direction and might have more points on one side than the other.

Chapter 2

EQUIPMENT

Learn about types of arrows and bows, kissers, releases, and other accessories.

Bows and arrows can be made of different types of materials. Most modern bows are made of wood, metal, or composite materials. Most arrows are made of aluminum or carbon fiber. Wood arrows are sometimes used by archers who enjoy using traditional-style equipment. Some wood arrows are made of cedar.

Arrows

Bowhunters use different types of tips on their arrows. Blunts are tips that are not sharp or pointed. They can be used to hunt small animals, such as wild turkey. Broadheads are sharp tips with blades. They are used for hunting large animals, such as deer or bear.

tip—the arrow's point

A bowhunter aims an arrow with a broadhead tip.

Fletchings keep an arrow steady while it flies. Fletchings are feathers or plastic vanes at the back of the arrow. Feathers are lighter than plastic vanes when they are dry. But plastic vanes will not absorb water when it rains. Fletchings can be 3, 4, or 5 inches (8, 10, or 13 centimeters) long.

The main part of an arrow is the shaft. This long tube connects the tip to the fletchings.

The plastic tip with a notch at the back end of an arrow is called the nock. The nock holds the arrow in place on the bowstring. As soon as the hunter lets go of the bowstring, the arrow flies forward. Without the nock, an arrow would fall to the ground when the archer pulled back the string.

EDGE FACT

An arrow launches off the bowstring at well over 200 feet (61 meters) per second.

fletchings—the vanes at the back of an arrow

Arrow Parts

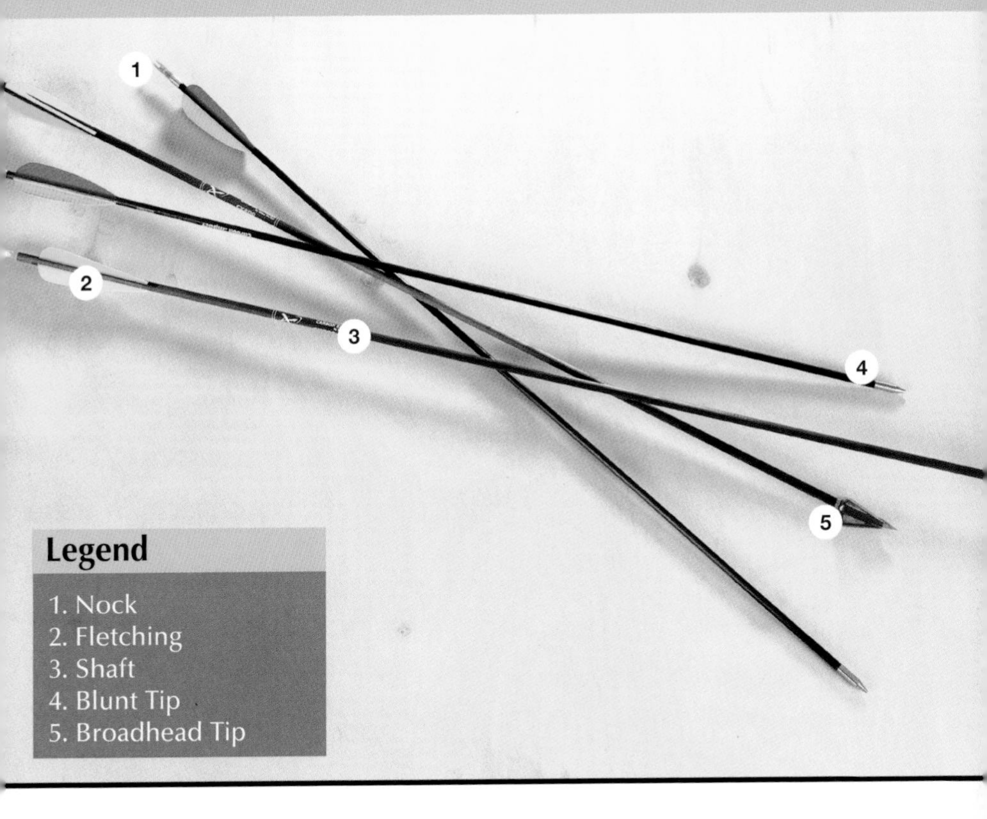

Bow Styles

Bowhunters use either a compound bow, a recurve bow, or a longbow. Even though these bows look different from one another, they all have a handle, a string, and limbs.

Bow Styles

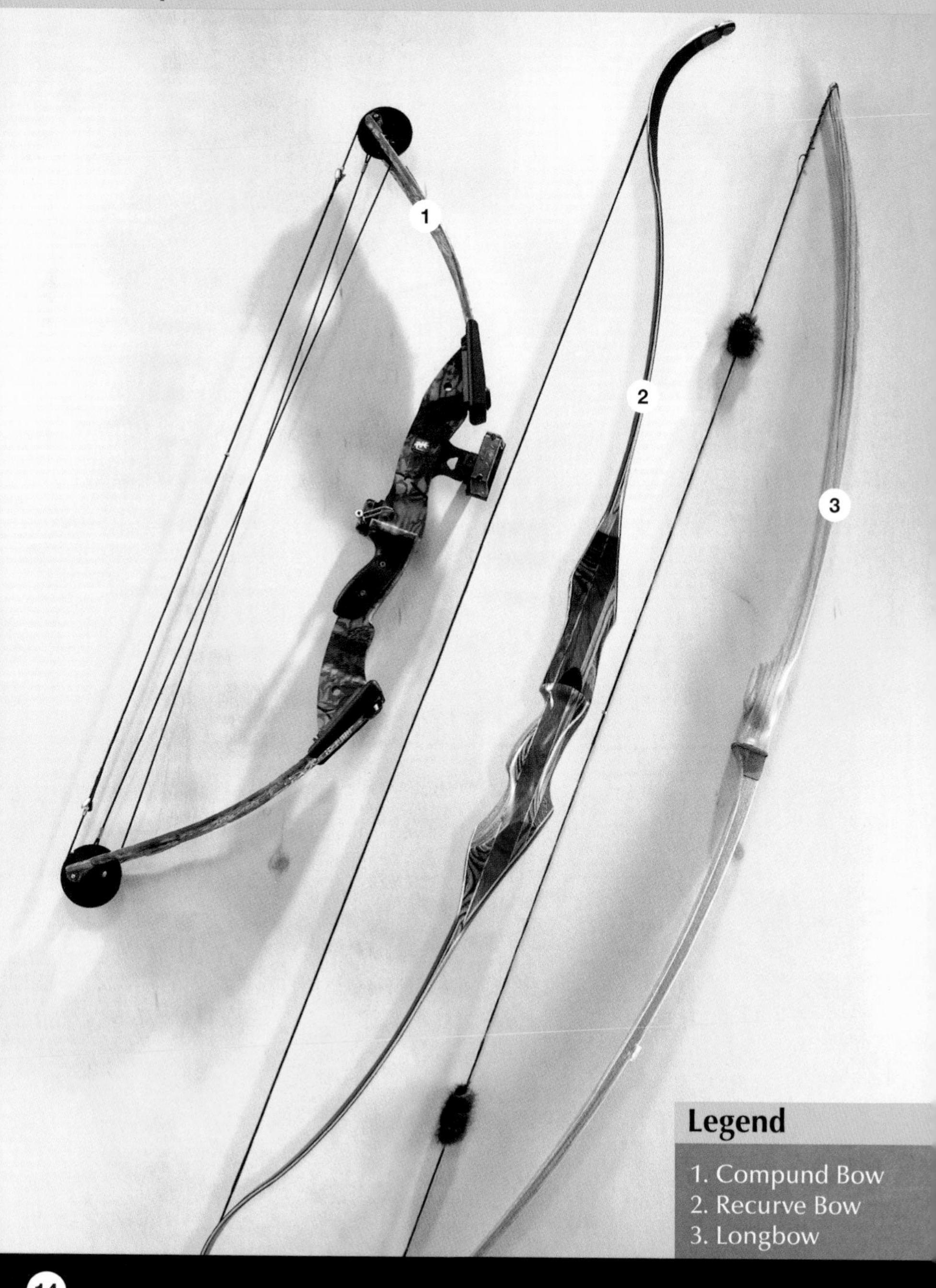

Legend

1. Compund Bow
2. Recurve Bow
3. Longbow

Hunters have to hold the bowstring back for a long time. Compound bows have cams. These round or oval wheels are on the top and bottom of the bow. They act like a pulley system and make it easier for hunters to hold the string while it is pulled back.

Recurve bows look different from compound bows. Recurve bows' limbs are bent forward, away from the hunter. Recurve bows are thick at the center. Hunters grip this area when they pull the bowstring.

Longbows look similar to recurve bows. Longbows are lightweight. Bow makers often carve longbows from one piece of wood.

Bow Accessories

Bowhunters place kissers on the bowstring. Hunters use kissers to make sure the bowstring is pulled back to the same position every time the bow is drawn. When the bowstring is pulled back, the kisser should touch the hunter's lips. If it touches the same place every time, the bowhunter will be more likely to shoot accurately each time.

kisser—a device that helps hunters pull the bowstring back to the same position every time

Many bowhunters use a release to pull the string back. Most releases wrap around the hunter's wrist and attach to the bowstring. Hunters do not hurt their fingers on the string when they use a release. The arrow shoots when a bowhunter lets go of a trigger on the release.

A quiver attaches to the bow and holds arrows. Some quivers can be worn on the hip or over the shoulder. Bowhunters can easily reach into their quivers to get more arrows.

Taking Care of a Bow

Hunters must take care of their bows to keep them in good condition. The strings and cables need to be waxed often. Bowhunters apply bowstring wax to keep the bowstring from being damaged by water.

EDGE FACT

H.W. Allen, a deer hunter from Missouri, invented the compound bow in the 1960s.

quiver—a container that holds arrows

A bowhunter uses a release to hold the bowstring.

Bowhunters check their bow for damage before using it. They make sure the string is not frayed. Hunters check for cracks by rubbing a cotton ball along the limbs of the bow. If there are cracks, the cotton will snag. Damaged bows have to be brought to a specialty shop for repair.

Essential Bowhunting Equipment

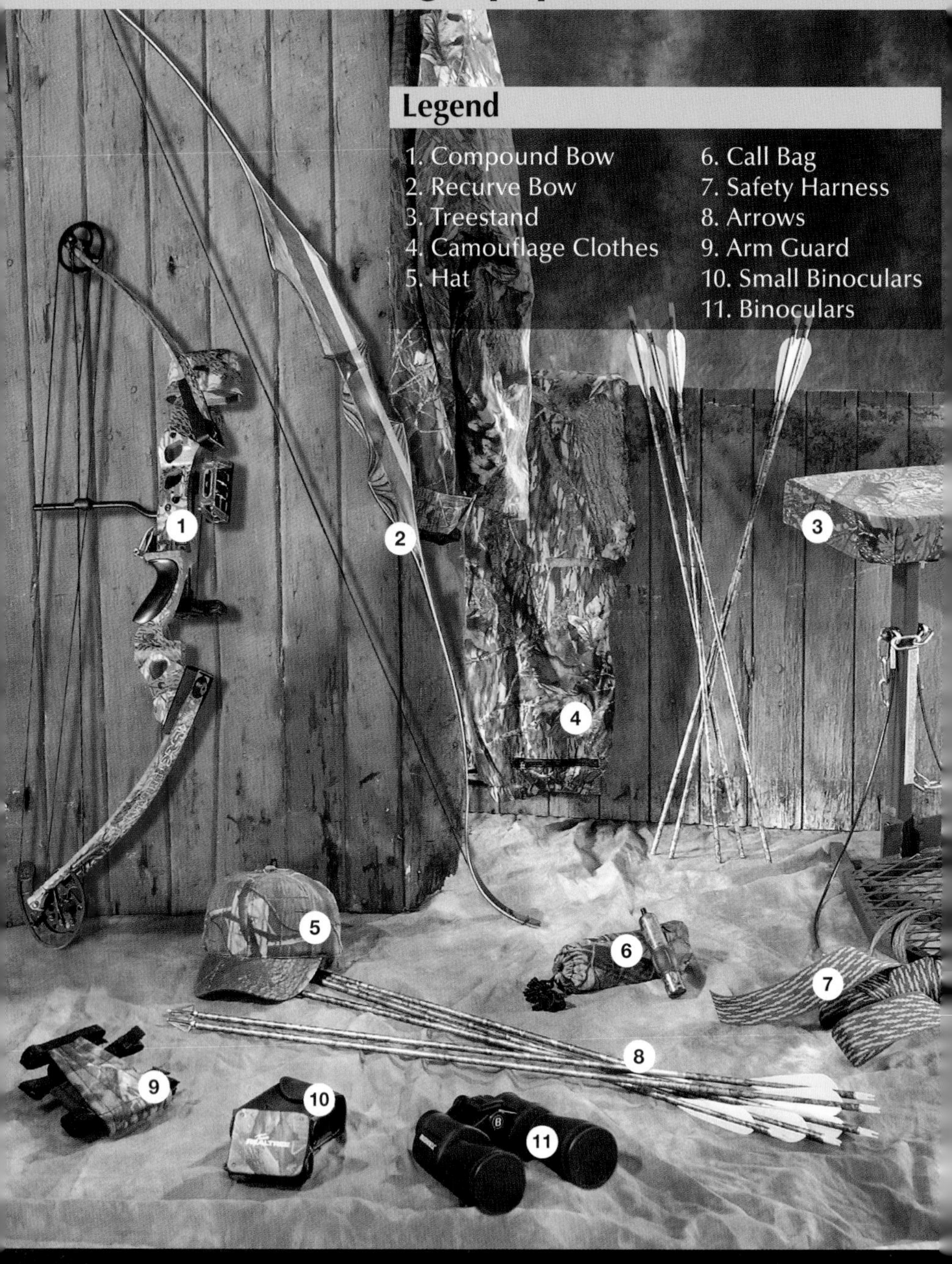

More Bowhunting Equipment

Before heading out on a hunt, bowhunters also need to bring a variety of other equipment.

- **First Aid Kit**—essential equipment in case of injury
- **Compass**—to know what direction you are facing
- **Binoculars**—to help hunters see their targets
- **Hunting Knife**—to clean out the internal organs from an animal after it has been killed; these organs could spoil the meat if they are left in the animal's body
- **Deer Scent**—for hunters to hide their scent; deer have a very good sense of smell
- **Stabilizer**—added to a bow to reduce noise and vibrations as an arrow is shot
- **Arm Guard**—protects a hunter's forearm from being scraped by the bowstring; the arm guard also holds back bulky clothing so it doesn't catch on the bowstring when shooting

EDGE FACT

Deer hunters use deer scents to attract bucks. One type of scent includes doe urine.

Clothing

Even a small noise can scare an animal away. Hunters wear clothing that doesn't make noise when they move.

Hunters' clothing should be warm in cold weather. Hunters wear extra layers. Fleece is a warm material. Hunters wear hats, coats, gloves, and wool socks in cold weather.

Many hunters wear camouflage clothing. These clothes are dyed with colors that blend with the colors of trees, grass, and snow. Camouflage clothing makes it harder for animals to see hunters.

Many states have laws about the colors of clothing that hunters wear. Some state laws say that all hunters need to wear bright orange clothing in the woods. Bright orange clothing allows hunters to see each other and not mistake hunters for animals.

camouflage—coloring that helps hunters blend in with their surroundings

Some bowhunters wear clothing that blends with their surroundings.

Chapter 3

Skills and Techniques

Learn about setting up a treestand, hunting techniques, and blinds.

Many bowhunters have favorite techniques they use to get close to their prey. Hunters want to make sure that they have the best chance of hitting the animal they are hunting.

Treestands

Treestands are raised platforms attached to a tree. Hunters sit in treestands while looking for prey. Animals are less likely to see hunters in a treestand.

Hunters need to know how to use a treestand safely. They practice shooting their bow from a raised position before using a treestand in the woods. They also must wear a safety harness.

Most hunters use portable treestands. With a portable stand, they can easily move from one tree to another.

A hunter in a treestand wears a safety harness.

Rattling

Hunters use different ways to attract the attention of deer. Rattling is one technique that hunters use to call bucks, or male deer. A hunter may use old antlers from a deer or antlers made of plastic.

The hunter takes one set of antlers in each hand and clicks them together. This rattling sound is like two bucks fighting. The sound attracts other bucks to the area.

Calling

Hunters make sounds to attract animals. A hunter might make a grunting noise. If the noise is similar to the sound that deer make, the hunter may attract deer.

A hunter may also blow into a tube to attract animals. The tubes are called "calls." Calls are made that sound like deer, turkeys, or other animals.

call—a device that makes a sound like the animal being hunted

Bowhunters click antlers together to attract bucks.

Hunters try to be still and quiet while stalking.

Stalking

Hunters walk through the woods looking for deer or other animals to stalk. They walk very slowly and try to be as quiet as possible.

Stalking is a difficult hunting technique. Most animals can hear very well. Even though hunters think they are being quiet, they might make sounds that only animals can hear.

Decoys

A bowhunter looking for wild turkey, deer, antelope, or elk may set up decoys. These wood or plastic animals look like real animals. Bowhunters have a better shot at animals that are still. A deer that sees a decoy might approach it and stand still near the decoy.

Blinds

Many hunters use different types of blinds. Blinds help hide hunters on the ground. Some hills, trees, and brush are natural blinds. Bowhunters hide behind these objects. Hunters may also cover themselves with leaves and branches.

blind—a covering where bowhunters hide

Many hunters buy portable blinds. These blinds might include a small shelter or a wall painted camouflage colors. Hunters set up blinds near areas where animals go to eat.

Hunters try their blinds at different locations. If no animals approach the blind, the hunter moves the blind to another hunting site.

Some hunters check for sites before they hunt. They watch for deer, bear, or turkey. They then set up their blind the night before they go hunting.

EDGE FACT

A bow and arrow can even be used to catch fish. The sport is called bowfishing.

Country Style Venison Stew

Serves: 4 *Children should have adult supervision.*

Ingredients:

½ pound (225 grams) bacon
2 pounds (910 grams) venison steak
4 tablespoons (60 mL) flour
6 cups (1,440 mL) water or beef broth
1 large tomato, chopped
2 medium carrots, sliced
2 medium stalks celery, sliced
2 medium potatoes, cut into 1-inch (2.5-centimeter) cubes
12 small white onions
1 tablespoon (15 mL) chopped parsley
1 cup (240 mL) fresh green peas
salt and pepper

Equipment:

knife
large saucepan
spoon
liquid measuring cup

What You Do:

1. Cut bacon into 1-inch (2.5-centimeter) cubes and cook in large saucepan until lightly browned. Remove bacon and set aside.
2. Cut venison into 2-inch (5-centimeter) pieces and brown over high heat in bacon drippings.
3. Stir in flour. Lower heat and let brown 2 to 3 minutes, stirring several times.
4. Add water or beef broth and simmer 1 hour or more until venison begins to get tender. Add more liquid as necessary.
5. Add all the other ingredients and continue to simmer to make a thick stew.

Chapter 4

CONSERVATION

Learn about hunting seasons, limits, and licenses.

In the early 1800s, millions of bison lived in the United States. By the end of that century, there were only 400 bison left. Hunters had killed too many of them. Deer and bighorn sheep were also overhunted. These animals were in danger of dying out because there were no laws to protect them.

Bowhunters help protect animals. They obey laws and work to keep the outdoors clean and free of pollution. They help conserve natural resources.

Hunting Laws

Today's hunting laws help to protect animals from being overhunted. Hunting regulations protect habitats and preserve the animal populations. These laws include setting daily and seasonal limits. Bowhunting seasons generally occur between September and November in the United States.

National programs protect endangered animals.

Some laws determine the kind or number of animals a hunter can shoot. A law might say that deer hunters can only shoot one buck and up to three does per season.

Other laws say what time of day hunters can hunt. Most states do not allow bowhunting before daylight or after dark. Hunters cannot see well in the woods at night. Hunting in the dark endangers other hunters. Also, an animal that should not be hunted could be accidentally shot.

Other laws protect endangered animals. Hunters cannot kill an animal whose population is in danger of dying out. Hunters should know which animals are endangered. Hunters who kill endangered animals can be sent to jail or never be allowed to hunt again.

endangered—in danger of dying out

Bowhunters are allowed to shoot only a certain number of bucks or does each season.

Conservation programs protect young animals from being hunted.

Keeping the Outdoors Clean

The outdoors is a place for all people to enjoy. People who spend time outdoors should respect the environment.

Hunters should clean up after themselves. They should follow the "leave no trace" rule. When hunters leave the woods, the area should look like they were never there at all.

Wildlife Conservation

Many groups in the United States are involved in protecting wildlife. Two of these groups are the U.S. Fish and Wildlife Service and the National Audubon Society. These groups teach people about wildlife conservation. They also plan conservation programs that offer safe areas for young and endangered animals to live.

National parks are also involved in wildlife conservation. They were created to protect wildlife and their habitats. People are not allowed to hunt in national parks. Many animals that are hard to find elsewhere can be seen in national parks.

Each state has wildlife conservation programs. The fees that states collect for hunting licenses often pay for activities that protect land and wildlife.

The Pittman-Robertson Act of 1937 is a federal law that taxes hunting equipment. The money from this tax funds wildlife research and the improvement of wildlife habitat.

Chapter 5

SAFETY

Learn about treestand harnesses, arrow safety, and bowhunting classes.

Bowhunting can be dangerous. Bowhunters must know and follow safety rules. Bowhunters also need to know how to use hunting equipment safely.

Treestand Safety

Hunters check their treestands for damage before putting them in a tree. They also check the tree where the stand will be placed. They make sure that the stand will not damage the tree. The tree should also be strong enough to hold the hunter.

Hunters wear safety harnesses while in a treestand. The harness is attached to the tree above the treestand. If hunters slip, the harness stops them from falling below the treestand.

Bowhunters check their treestand before climbing.

Hunters do not climb trees while holding their bow and arrows. If they fall, they could land on an arrow. Hunters climb to the treestand first. They use ropes called haul lines to pull up their equipment once they have the safety harness on.

Being Responsible with Arrows

Bowhunters check their arrows before shooting. A damaged arrow can be dangerous. A broken arrow could snap back and injure the bowhunter when the string is pulled.

Hunters make sure a target can be seen before shooting. If an arrow is carelessly shot into the air, it could come back down and hit the hunter or someone else.

Hunters should never point an arrow at a target that they do not want to shoot. Hunters need to be aware of what might be behind their target. They should not shoot if they are not sure of what the arrow could strike if they miss.

A bowhunter uses a haul line to lift and lower a bow and arrows to the treestand.

Many scouting groups teach basic archery skills.

Safety Training

Bowhunters need safety training before they hunt. Many experienced bowhunters take courses to learn about new hunting laws. Scouting groups offer many bowhunting and archery courses.

All states offer bowhunting safety courses. Many hunting laws are taught in bowhunting safety classes. Hunters have to obey these laws and use good technique.

Some states have a minimum age requirement for a person requesting a bowhunting license. Most states say that a hunter must be 14 years old. Young bowhunters should check with wildlife agencies in their state to learn about hunting safety courses.

Good hunters have both hunting skills and safety knowledge. These hunters know that proper equipment and safety are important for hunters, animals, and the environment. Good bowhunters come prepared for their adventures in the outdoors.

EDGE FACT

Many states require that bowhunters complete a bowhunting education course before they can buy a bowhunting license.

Mule Deer

Description: Mule deer are gray-brown. They have a narrow white tail with a black tip. Some mule deer have a white patch on their throat or chin. Mule deer are known for their large, fuzzy ears. Male mule deer weigh up to 400 pounds (181 kilograms). Females weigh up to 200 pounds (91 kilograms).

Habitat: woods, grassy areas, mountains, river valleys

Food: grasses, leaves

White-tailed Deer

Description: White-tailed deer are red-brown. Their tails are brown and white. The underside of the tail is completely white. These deer also have white patches on their nose, throat, and around their eyes. Male white-tailed deer weigh up to 300 pounds (136 kilograms). Females weigh up to 200 pounds (91 kilograms).

Habitat: woods, grassy area

Food: grasses, leaves

American Black Bear

Description: Not all American black bears are completely black. Some are brown, and some have white patches on their chest. Black bears can run up to 25 miles (40 kilometers) per hour. They can grow to be 5 feet (1.5 meters) long and weigh between 200 to 500 pounds (91 to 227 kilograms).

Habitat: forests in northern United States, Canada

Food: mice, squirrels, fish, bird eggs, berries, fruit, nuts, leaves, roots

Wild Turkey

Description: Wild turkeys have long legs and a long neck. They have dark feathers. They also have very small heads. Males have bronze-colored feathers. Female turkeys have light brown feather tips on the front part of their body. Male turkeys weigh up to 16 pounds (7 kilograms). Females weigh about 9 pounds (4 kilograms).

Habitat: forests, wooded and grassy areas

Food: insects, seeds, small nuts, fruits

GLOSSARY

archery (AR-chuh-ree)—the sport of shooting at targets using a bow and arrow

camouflage (KAM-uh-flahzh)—coloring that makes hunters blend in with their surroundings

composite (kuhm-POZ-it)—made up of many parts from different sources

endangered (en-DAYN-jurd)—at risk of dying out

habitat (HAB-uh-tat)—the place and natural conditions in which animals live

prehistoric (pree-hi-STOR-ik)—from a time before history was recorded

quiver (KWIV-ur)—a container for arrows

stalking (STAWK-ing)—hunting or tracking an animal as quietly as possible

technique (tek-NEEK)—a way of doing something that requires skill

READ MORE

Lewis, Joan. *Hunting*. Get Going! Hobbies. Chicago: Heinemann Library, 2006.

Wilson, Jef. *Hunting for Fun!* For Fun! Minneapolis, Minn.: Compass Point Books, 2006.

INTERNET SITES

FactHound offers a safe, fun way to find Internet sites related to this book. All of the sites on FactHound have been researched by our staff.

Here's how:

1. Visit *www.facthound.com*
2. Choose your grade level.
3. Type in this book ID **1429608145** for age-appropriate sites. You may also browse subjects by clicking on letters, or by clicking pictures and words.
4. Click on the **Fetch It** button.

FactHound will fetch the best sites for you!

WWW.FACTHOUND.COM®

INDEX